ANCIENT ARCTIC MAMMALS

WRITTEN BY
Dana Hopkins

ILLUSTRATED BY
Aaron Edzerza

T0124459

INTRODUCTION

Many different kinds of mammals live in Canada's Arctic today. These include seals, wolves, beavers, caribou, *siksiit*,* and polar bears.

The **ancestors** of some of these animals lived here a long, long time ago. Some were here even before humans!

ancestors: early types of animals or plants that others have descended from.

***siksiit** (sik-SEET): plural of siksik, or ground squirrel

3

Today, winter in the Arctic is long and very cold. In some places, snow and ice build up for 10 months of the year. During the short summer, plants grow close to the ground.

But the land wasn't always like this. Thousands, perhaps even millions of years ago, it looked very different. During certain periods, temperatures were even colder than today. During others, they were warmer. There were swamps in some places and trees in others, and more ponds and lakes than there are now.

The ancestors of the animals we know today looked and behaved differently in this different environment.

SEAL ANCESTORS

Seals have been an important part of life in the Arctic for thousands of years.

Seals are related to an ancient **extinct** animal called Puijila. Puijila looked a little bit like a seal and a little bit like a river otter. It was just over 1 metre long from nose to tail.

Puijila had legs instead of flippers, and it probably had webbed feet like a goose. It could swim and walk.

extinct: a species of animal that no longer exists.

Puijila had strong jaws and sharp teeth, so it would have been able to crunch and tear its prey. It probably ate lots of fish.

Just like seals today, it had huge eyes that helped it see when it was swimming. It had long whiskers that it used to feel for fish in deep, dark water. It probably had fur that kept it warm on land and in the water.

Puijila lived 20 to 24 million years ago in the High Arctic. Back then, temperatures were warmer than they are today. There were more lakes, too.

The first skeleton of a Puijila was found on Devon Island in a place where a lake used to be. This tells scientists that Puijila was a freshwater animal, unlike today's seals, which live in the saltwater ocean.

Did You Know?

The Puijila is what scientists call a "missing link." Very early ancestors of the seal walked on land, and today's seals live in the ocean. Puijila is the link between the two, because it lived both on land and in the water.

DIRE WOLVES

In the Arctic today, you will find black wolves and grey wolves. These large members of the dog family are hunters that move very fast.

Long ago, a different species of wolf lived in the Arctic. This gigantic wolf was called a dire wolf. It is the largest species of wolf to have ever lived.

Dire wolves looked like today's grey wolves, but they were larger and heavier, with bigger heads. They were about 1.5 metres long from nose to tail and weighed almost 70 kilograms.

Dire wolves lived 125 000 to 9500 years ago. They probably died out at the end of the last **ice age**, when the climate warmed up again.

ice age: a time when thick ice sheets called glaciers cover huge areas of land.

Dire wolves hunted in packs, just like wolves today. But unlike wolves today, dire wolves didn't chase their prey. Instead, they waited to surprise and attack their prey. The pack worked together to kill the prey animal.

Scientists think dire wolves would have been able to kill big animals, including bison and horses. Their massive jaws and teeth gave them a deadly bite. They could crunch through bones to get to the marrow inside.

GIANT BEAVERS

Today, beavers live in most areas of North America, including parts of the Arctic.

Millions of years ago, giant beavers lived in the Arctic. These are the ancestors of today's beavers. The oldest known fossil of a giant beaver is three million years old. **Fossils** have been found in Yukon and farther south, in Ontario and New Brunswick. Giant beavers lived in lakes, ponds, or swamps.

fossils: the remains or traces of plants and animals that lived long ago, especially the hard parts, like shells or bones.

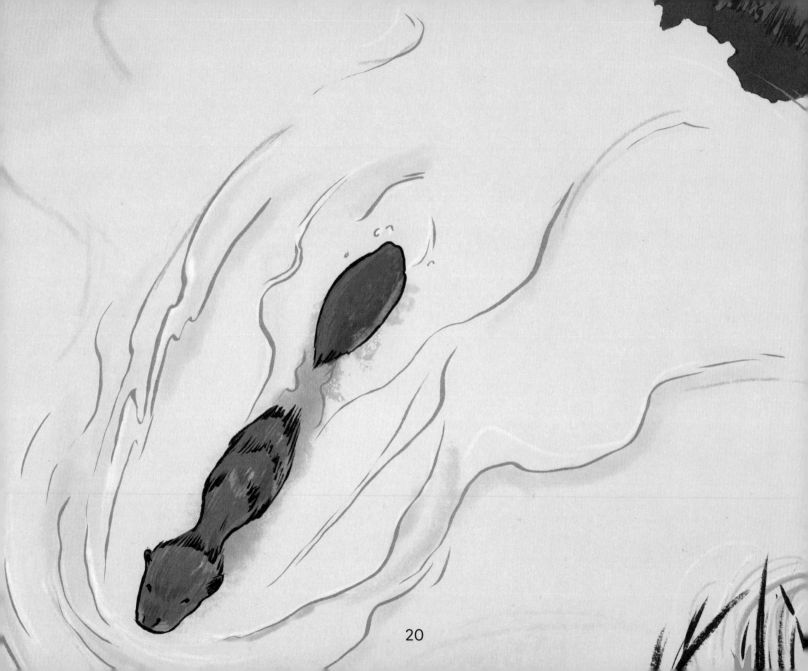

Giant beavers were 2 metres long from nose to tail. That's about the same as a female polar bear. They were about 1 metre tall, and they weighed up to 200 kilograms, which is heavier than a caribou.

They had a narrower tail than beavers today, and much larger teeth.

The giant beaver was a herbivore, which means it ate plants and did not eat meat. Today, beavers use their sharp teeth to cut down trees. By studying the fossils of giant beaver teeth, scientists can tell these ancestors did not cut down trees. Instead, they used their teeth to tear up plants that grew in the water.

ANCIENT CARIBOU

Caribou have lived in the Arctic for 1.6 million years. Even though most large animals that lived during the last ice age died out around 10 000 years ago, caribou survived. Caribou today look and act a lot like their ancient relatives.

23

Did You Know?

Scientists have found weapons preserved in ice that were used to hunt caribou about 9000 years ago. Ancient hunters climbed up high on mountains and hunted caribou moving below.

Ancient caribou lived in areas that were grassy in the summer and snowy in the winter. They lived in herds, just as they do today.

Like caribou today, ancient caribou migrated to find food: grasses in the summer and lichens in the winter.

ANCIENT SIKSIIT

Just like caribou, siksiit today are a lot like the ones that lived millions of years ago.

Siksiit, also called Arctic ground squirrels, have lived in North America for 10 million years. Today, you will find them all over the Arctic.

Remains of ancient siksiit have been found in Alaska and Yukon. Ancient siksiit made burrows and hibernated, just like siksiit do today. Gold miners often find these burrows **preserved** in the permafrost.

preserved: kept in its original state.

Inuit tell stories about the nanurluk, a giant polar bear that roams the North. Maybe the nanurluk and the king polar bear are the same creature!

28

GIANT BEARS

The polar bear might be the most well-known animal that lives in the Arctic today. In times long ago, other bears also lived in the Arctic.

A polar bear ancestor called the king polar bear roamed the Arctic 130 000 years ago. Not very much is known about it. Scientists found a skull that might have belonged to the king polar bear. They also found a piece of bone from a king polar bear's leg. From that bone, they can make guesses about what the bear was like.

Scientists think that the king polar bear probably had the same kind of skeleton as a grizzly bear, but might have been better adapted to the cold, like a polar bear. That means that polar bears and grizzly bears might both be related to this ancient ancestor.

This bear might have been able to hunt large prey, like bison and mammoths, an extinct relative of the elephant. It might also have been a scavenger, scaring away other animals from their kills and taking the food for themselves.

Another kind of bear that once lived in the North was the giant short-faced bear. The giant short-faced bear was not only one of the biggest bears in history; it was one of the biggest mammal predators ever.

Giant short-faced bears weighed between 500 and 1000 kilograms, about the same as a walrus. They were 2 metres long and had very long legs. When they stood up on their back legs, they would have been between 3 and 4 metres tall!

Can you imagine a beaver the size of a polar bear roaming the tundra? What about a seal that can walk on land? These animals and more lived in the Arctic long ago.

What other kinds of animals do you think might have lived here?

Nunavummi